STATE
GOVERNMENTS

A DECLARATION

of RIGHTS, and PLAN of Government for the State of
New-Hampshire.

WHEREAS by the tyrannical Administration of the Government of the King and Parliament of Great-Britain, this State of New-Hampshire, with the other United-States of AMERICA, have been necessitated to reject the British Government, and declare themselves INDEPENDENT STATES ; all which is more largely set forth by the CONTINENTAL CONGRESS, in their Resolution or Declaration of the fourth of July A. D. 1776.

AND WHEREAS, it is recommended by the said CONTINENTAL CONGRESS to each and every of the said United-States to establish a FORM OF GOVERNMENT most conducive to the Welfare thereof. We the DELEGATES of the said State of NEW-HAMPSHIRE chosen for the Purpose of forming a permanent PLAN of GOVERNMENT subject to the Revisal of our CONSTITUENTS, have composed the following DECLARATION of RIGHTS, and PLAN of GOVERNMENT ; and recommend the same to our CONSTITUENTS for their Approbation.

A DECLARATION of the RIGHTS of the PEOPLE of the STATE of NEW-HAMPSHIRE.

First. WE declare, that we the People of the State of New-Hampshire, are Free and Independant of the Crown of Great-Britain.

Secondly. We the People of this State, are intitled to Life, Liberty, and Property ; and all other Immunities and Privileges which we heretofore enjoyed.

Thirdly. The Common and Statute Laws of England, adopted and used here ; and the Laws of this State (not inconsistent with said Declaration of INDEPENDENCE) now are, and shall be in force here, for the Welfare and good Government of the State, unless the same shall be repealed or altered by the future Legislature thereof.

Fourthly. The whole and intire Power of Government of this State, is vested in, and must be derived from the People thereof, and from no other Source whatsoever.

Fifthly. The future Legislature of this State, shall make no Laws to infringe the Rights of Conscience, or any other of the natural, unalienable Rights of Men, or contrary to the Laws of GOD, or against the Protestant Religion.

Sixthly. The Extent of Territory of this State, is, and shall be the same which was under the Government of the late Governor *John Wentworth,* Esq; Governor of *New-Hampshire.* Reserving nevertheless, our Claim to the *New-Hampshire Grants,* so called, situate to the West of Connecticut River.

Seventhly. The Right of Trial by Jury in all Cases as heretofore used in this State, shall be preserved inviolate forever.

A PLAN of Government for the State of New-Hampshire.

First. THE State of *New-Hampshire* shall be governed by a COUNCIL, and House of REPRESENTATIVES, to be chosen as here in after mentioned, and to be stiled the GENERAL COURT of the State of *New-Hampshire.*

Second. The COUNCIL shall consist for the present of twelve Members, to be elected out of the several Counties in the State, in Proportion to their respective Number of Inhabitants.

Third. The Numbers belonging to each County for the present, according to said Proportion being as followeth, viz.—To the County of Rockingham, five—to the County of Strafford, two---to the County of Hillsborough, two---to the County of Cheshire, two---to the County of Grafton, one

Fourth. The number for the County of Rockingham, shall not be increased or diminished hereafter, but remain the same ; and the Numbers for the other Counties shall be increased or deminished as their aforesaid Proportion to the County of Rockingham may chance to vary.

Fifth. The House of REPRESENTATIVES shall be chosen as follows. Every Town or Parish, choosing Town Officers, amounting to one hundred Families, and upwards, shall send one Representative for each hundred Families they consist of, (or such lesser Number as they please) or class themselves with some other Towns or Parishes that will join in sending a Representative.

Sixth. All other Towns and Parishes under the number of one hundred Families, shall have Liberty to class themselves together to make the number of one hundred Families or upwards, and being so classed, each Class shall send one Representative.

Seventh. The number of COUNCILLORS belonging to each County shall be ascertained and done by the General-Court every Time there is a new Proportion made of the State Tax which shall be once in seven Years at the least, and oftner if need be.

Eighth. All the Male Inhabitants of the State of lawful Age, paying Taxes, and professing the Protestant Religion, shall be deemed legal Voters in choosing COUNCILLORS and REPRESENTATIVES, and having an Estate of Three Hundred Pounds equal to Silver at six Shillings and eight Pence per Ounce, one half at least whereof to be real Estate, and lying within this State, with the Qualifications aforesaid, shall be capable of being elected.

Ninth. The Selectmen of each respective Town and Parish, choosing Town Officers containing one hundred Families or upwards, and also of each respective Class of Towns classed together as aforesaid, shall notify the legal Voters of their respective Towns, Parishes, or Classes, qualified as aforesaid, in the usual Way of notifying Town-Meetings, giving fifteen Days notice at least, to meet at some convenient Place on the last Wednesday of November annually, to choose COUNCILLORS and REPRESENTATIVES.

Tenth. And the Voters being met, and the Moderator chosen, shall proceed to choose their Representative or Repepresentatives, required by this Constitution by a Majority of the Voters present, who shall be notified accordingly; and a Return thereof made into the Secretary's Office, by the first Wednesday of January then next.

Eleventh. And such Representatives shall be paid their Wages by their Constituents, and for their Travel by the State.

Twelfth. And in the Choice of COUNCILLORS each Voter shall deliver his Vote to the Moderator for the number of COUNCILLORS respectively required, with the Word COUNCILLORS written thereon, & the Voters Name endorsed to prevent Duplicity.

Thirteenth. These Votes shall be sealed up by the Moderator, and transmitted by the Constable to one of the Justices of the Inferior Court of Common Pleas for the County, before the second Wednesday in December next following.

The New Hampshire Constitution

STATE GOVERNMENTS

by Barbara Silberdick Feinberg

Franklin Watts
A First Book
New York ★ Chicago ★ London ★ Sydney

Dedication

In memory of my husband, Gerald Feinberg (1933–1992), who first suggested that I write books for young people. With infinite patience, he taught me to use a word processor and often helped me to locate research materials. Most of all, he gave me encouragement and love.

Photographs copyright ©: American Antiquarian Society, 2; MacDonald Photography/Photri, 8; Richard Hutchings/PhotoEdit, 10; Robert Brenner/PhotoEdit, 13, 50 (bottom); AP/Wide World, 16, 26; The Bettmann Archive, 23; David Jennings/The Image Works, 29; David Young-Wolf/PhotoEdit, 33; Tom McCarthy/PhotoEdit, 36; Jim Pickerell/Tony Stone Worldwide, 39; Bob Daemmrich/The Image Works, 40; Elena Rooraid/PhotoEdit, 43; MacDonald Photography/Photri, 46 (top); David R. Frazier Photolibrary, 46 (bottom), 52; UPI/Bettmann, 49; Lizabeth J. Menzies/The Image Works, 50 (top).

Library of Congress Cataloging-in-Publication Data

Feinberg, Barbara Silberdick.
State governments / by Barbara Silberdick Feinberg.
p. cm. (First book)
Includes bibliographical references and index.
Summary: Examines what governors, legislators, judges,
    and other state officials do, and how their powers and
    responsibilities differ from state to state.
ISBN 0-531-20154-6 (hc : lib. bdg.)
1. State governments—United States—Juvenile literature.
[1.State governments.] I. Title II. Series.
JK2408.F37 1993
353.9 dc20
92-27368 CIP AC

Table of Contents

Acknowledgements

I would like to thank the following individuals and their staffs for contributing materials to this books: Vincent Di Figlia, Judge, the Superior Court of California, County of San Diego; Harry Fritz, Montana State Senator; Lou Patten, Tennessee State Senator; Barbara Roberts, Governor of Oregon; and Menasha Tausner, Deputy Public Advocate, New Jersey Department of the Public Advocate.

For helping me to prepare this book, I am indebted to three editors at Franklin Watts, Inc.: Reni Roxas, who conceived the idea to do this project; Lorna Greenberg, who gave me excellent suggestions and support during a difficult time; and E. Russell Primm III, who actually transformed the manuscript into a book.

I received invaluable assistance from Anna Bunshaft, my aunt; Gina Cane, a teacher in the Larchmont school system and a cherished friend; Michael Neft, Connecticut College Class of 1993, my researcher; and as always, Gerald Feinberg, my husband.

A Note to Readers

State government takes many actions that affect your lives. For example, governors, legislatures, departments, and agencies make rulings about which holidays you are let out of school, the number of days you must attend school each year, what types of tests you take, and the training your teachers receive. They also make laws concerning the quality of the air you breathe and the water you drink. Can you think of some other examples?

As you read the pages of this book, you will be introduced to the state governments at work. You will learn what state officials do and how their powers and responsibilities differ from state to state. Some of the words you read are printed in bold type. These words may not be familiar to you, so you may want to look in the Glossary to find out what they mean. They will help you to become an informed citizen who may even hold an office in state government some day.

The State Capitol building in Lincoln, Nebraska

Chapter One

S TATE GOVERNMENTS

A Variety of Constitutional Duties

Before the United States of America came into being, thirteen separate American states managed their own affairs. Although they did join together in a league, they were too jealous of one another to give up their independence. Finally, in 1787 they drew up a **Constitution**, which united them in one strong national government. This written agreement defined the duties and limited the powers of the new government. It also formed a special partnership between the states and the national government, known as **federalism**.

Most young people will deal directly with state governments when they apply for their drivers' licenses.

Federalism divides power between the national and state governments. In some matters, such as taxing citizens, the states and the national government share powers. The Constitution, however, makes the national government's laws supreme, superior to state laws, so states may not take actions that conflict with the national government. If the Constitution didn't declare national government laws superior to state laws, people would not always know which laws to obey. In other matters, each government exercises its own independent powers. For example, only the national government can print and coin money and set up post offices. Only the states can issue drivers' licenses and birth certificates.

Between 1788 and 1959, thirty-seven states joined the original thirteen and became members of the United States of America. As partners in the federal system, the states take part in national elections. The Constitution allows states to set their own time, place, and method for electing lawmakers to the national legislature. Thus the states have different voting procedures. The national government, however, has stepped in when a state's election rules have proven unreasonable or unfair and kept certain groups of people from voting. The Constitution also requires the states to come together every four years to form an **electoral college** which helps elect the president after the voters have chosen their winner.

The Constitution also describes the way states must treat each other. They are encouraged to return criminals who have escaped from other states so fugitives are punished for their crimes. States must also accept court judgments, records, and documents from other states. For example, a birth certificate registered in Hawaii is valid proof of identity in Texas. Without this requirement, it would be difficult for individuals to conduct business or have their marriages and divorces recognized outside their home state.

In addition, states must offer visitors from other states the same rights their own residents enjoy, or else people traveling from one state to another might feel as if they were visiting a foreign country. Americans visiting any state have the right to be protected by state laws, to hold a job, to bring a lawsuit in the state's courts, and to be taxed at the same rates as residents. Before giving visitors the full benefits of state citizenship, however, a state may require newcomers to live in the state for a minimum amount of time; this is called a **residency requirement**. States may also require drivers to be retested in order to have a state license. After all, each of the states has different traffic regulations and drivers should learn what they are.

An interstate compact between New Jersey and New York operates commuter transportation in New York City.

States also cooperate voluntarily in matters of common interest. With the approval of Congress, they set up **interstate compacts**. These agreements concern such matters as common management of waterways, transportation, and environmental protection. For example, the Port Authority of New York and New Jersey is in charge of the New York Harbor as well as the bridges and the tunnels that link the two states. States usually belong to twenty or so compacts.

Besides the rules set down in the national Constitution, the individual states must also follow the guidelines of their own state constitutions. This is not as difficult as it may seem. Most state constitutions are modeled on the national Constitution, except the constitutions of Massachusetts and New Hampshire, which were written before the United States was founded. Like the national Constitution, all state constitutions separate government into three parts: a **legislature**, to make laws; an **executive** to carry out laws; and a **judiciary**, courts where judges decide disputes about laws and try lawbreakers. All state constitutions contain a **Bill of Rights**, guaranteeing citizens' basic freedoms.

The state constitutions vary in length. Vermont's is the shortest at 6,600 words while Alabama's is longest at 174,000 words. By contrast, the original Constitution of the United States is only 4,550 words long. State constitutions are often much more detailed than the national constitution. They contain precise descriptions of what state officials may do and how they must go about doing it. In addition, they set up local governments for cities and rural areas. They also have been known to include trivial topics. For example, Georgia's constitution promises to reward the first person to discover oil within the state.

Because state constitutions are so detailed, they tend to become outdated and must be changed. Louisiana has written eleven new constitutions. States hold special meetings called **constitutional conventions** to completely rewrite their constitutions. More than 230 constitutional conventions have been held so far. For less sweeping changes, state governments pass **amendments** to add or to subtract from their constitutions. By 1990, California had amended its 1879 constitution more than 475 times.

State constitutions are just plans of government. State officials turn those plans into actions, and their powers differ from state to state. These governors, legislators, judges, and administrators must all solve the daily problems their citizens face and meet their responsibilities to the national government and the other states. The variety of solutions state officials devise can teach lessons to the rest of the country. With their special knowledge of local conditions and needs, these officials help make the state governments vital partners in the federal system.

Corretta Scott King, wife of the slain civil rights leader, Martin Luther King, Jr.

Chapter Two

STATE LEGISLATURES:

Many Different Lawmakers at Work

Since 1986, the national government has observed Martin Luther King, Jr.'s birthday as a holiday. Each state has the right to decide which days will be official state holidays, and in 1991, Montana became the forty-seventh state to set aside the third Monday in January to honor the late Dr. King, as well as minorities still struggling for equality. The Montana state legislature ordered schools, government offices, and banks closed throughout the state, and gave state workers the day off with pay. Not all the state legislatures pass the same laws. As late as 1990, Arizona voted against observing Martin Luther King, Jr.'s birthday. By January 1993, however, all fifty states decided to celebrate this holiday.

All state legislatures are not alike. Forty-nine states have two-house legislatures, called by such names as the General Court and General Assembly. They also come in different sizes. The New Hampshire House of Representatives has the most members (four hundred), while Alaska has the fewest (forty). The Minnesota Senate is largest with sixty-seven members, while Alaska's is the smallest with only twenty members.

Nebraska has only one house, a state senate. Nebraskans claim this system avoids delays and gives voters a clear idea of who is responsible for their laws. In the past, Georgia, Pennsylvania, and Vermont also had one-house legislatures. The other states insist the traditional two-house system is better because it requires legislators to study carefully and discuss proposed laws before acting, and it gives people more opportunities to offer their opinions about a law.

In seven states with small populations, the legislatures meet every other year. In the rest of the states, meetings are held every year. In about thirty-eight states, state constitutions limit the number of days the legislature meets (the average is sixty days). Because legislative sessions are so short, three-fourths of the legislators hold office as a part-time job. Many also work as lawyers.

There are other differences that affect the nation's 7,462 state legislators. Most state senators are elected for four-year terms, and most representatives for two-year terms. In some states, however, they both serve for the same length of time. In 1990, Oklahoma set a limit of twelve years on the amount of time state legislators could hold office; this was the first such term-limit regulation passed by any state (Colorado and California soon passed similar laws). By 1992, all the western states except New Mexico and Hawaii were deciding whether to let voters keep electing the same people to state and national offices every year.

As partners in the federal system, state legislatures divide the state's population into the congressional districts; each district elects a representative to the national legislature. Voters in each state also send two senators to Washington who are chosen in statewide elections. Every ten years, a national census counts how many people live in each state. If the population of a state has increased, it is given more congressional representatives at the expense of states whose population has shrunk. For example, as a result of the 1990 census, Texas gained three new representatives while New York lost three. As a result, state legislators in both states had to draw up **redistricting** plans to reflect these changes. They also adjust the boundaries of their own state legislative districts as required by state laws or state constitutions.

Governors must approve both national and state redistricting plans. Getting their consent may require some compromises if the governor and a majority of the legislature belong to different **political parties**. Political parties are organizations that get people to run for office in elections. The political party that elects the most members in the state legislature gains an advantage in future elections, as its legislative leaders draw district lines to take in most of the party's voters. This is why congressional and state election districts often have had strange shapes, looking like snakes or salamanders, rather than tidy squares or rectangles. As a result, some districts contained a few thousand voters while others contained ten times as many. Finally, in the 1960s, the courts insisted that every election district, regardless of its shape, must contain the same number of people so that each citizen's vote counts equally.

The main purpose of state legislatures is to pass laws. They have the power to raise or lower taxes and to determine how state funds will be spent. State parks, hospitals, schools, and prisons all depend on decisions the legislators make. Despite the differing structures of state legislatures, most follow similar procedures. Nearly half of the legislatures use **joint committees** to speed up their work. These committees, made up of members of both houses, screen out the weakest **bills** (proposed laws) and send the rest to be introduced in the legislature. The bills to be introduced are turned over to **standing committees**. These committees are permanent groups, divided by subject matter, that recommend whether the bills should be passed or rejected. They hold hearings, questioning experts, concerned individuals, and groups, thus giving the public a chance to speak out on bills being considered in the legislature. As a result of what committee members learn from the hearings, they may make changes in the bills. If a majority of the committee supports a revised bill, it is sent to the house for further discussion, changes, and a vote. If the bill passes, it is sent to the other house where it goes through the same process. If the two houses pass alternative versions of the same bill, they set up a **conference committee** made up of members from each house, to settle the differences. After passage by the state legislature, the compromise bill is sent to the governor for signature. Sometimes the public may approve or reject laws the legislature has passed by voting on them in a **referendum** at the next general election.

As partners in the **federal** system, state legislatures are sometimes asked to agree to proposed changes in the national Constitution. Although Congress (the national legislature) may suggest amendments, thirty-eight (or three-fourths) of the state legislatures must approve them. Not every amendment Congress suggests is accepted by the states. Only twenty-eight state legislatures agreed to a 1924 amendment to end child labor. In those days, many young children worked long hours in factories under terrible conditions. The states solved the problem by passing their own child labor laws and by requiring children to attend school for eight to twelve years. Because it is difficult to get thirty-eight very different states to agree to change the Constitution, only twenty-seven amendments have been passed in more than two hundred years.

State legislatures may also amend state constitutions. Not all states follow the same procedures. In Delaware, the legislators have the power both to suggest and consent to constitutional changes. In most states, however, the lawmakers may recommend an amendment for public approval at the next election. In 1990, Florida voters agreed to a constitutional amendment requiring a three-day waiting period before people who bought pistols could take them home. In all states, except Delaware, voters

Until states passed child labor laws in the early part of this century, many children worked long hours in factories under poor conditions.

must approve or reject proposed changes to state constitutions at the next election by means of a referendum. Seventeen states also allow their citizens to suggest amendments for voters to accept or reject at election time. These **initiative petitions** must contain signatures of from three to fifteen percent of all the people who voted in the last election. Initiatives are also used to propose new laws.

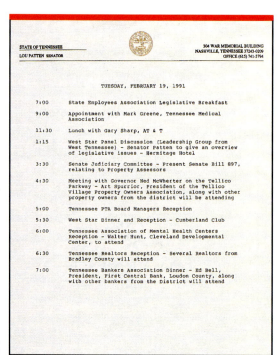

A day in Tennessee State Senator Lou Patten's schedule reveals a wide variety of tasks—legislative duties, meetings with community and business leaders, and personal appearances.

Legislatures have the power to make sure the executive branch of state government is performing its job properly. Lawmakers question state officials about their duties, afterwards may arrange to inspect such things as school bus safety, or how well industries are obeying state standards for clean air and water. Under **sunset laws**, legislators may require state agencies to explain why they shouldn't be eliminated after six or seven years. In this way state legislatures can dispose of useless projects and use the freed funds to set up new programs.

Legislators must also approve the individuals governors want to appoint as heads of state departments and agencies. If they find evidence of wrongdoing, legislatures have the power to remove officials from their posts through **impeachment**, a procedure that resembles a criminal trial. In 1988, Arizona lawmakers impeached Governor Evan Mecham. The Arizona House of Representatives charged him with improperly taking money from a state fund and with other wrongdoing. The state Senate then examined the evidence, found him guilty, and ordered him to leave office. He was the seventh American governor to be impeached. If the legislature had not removed him, Arizona voters would have had the chance to force him out of office in a special **recall** election.

State legislatures do their work in a variety of ways. After all, the people they represent in different parts of the country do not always share the same opinions, needs, or interests. While the legislatures are all partners in the same federal system, they make it possible for each state to go about its own business in its own way.

Governor Ann Richards of Texas

Chapter Three

EXECUTIVES:

Assorted Powers and Responsibilities

Americans have recently become familiar with many state governors through television commercials advertising various merits of their states. Cecil D. Andrus of Idaho has urged Americans to buy his state's potatoes, and Governor Jim Florio has praised the New Jersey shore as a vacation spot. Appearing in television ads, however, is not the only way governors promote their states' interests. They often visit Congress to appeal for funding or meet with foreign business leaders to encourage them to build factories in their states. As spokespersons for their states, there are many different ways for governors to do their jobs.

Governors are in frequent contact with state and national lawmakers, urging them to pass laws the governor feels are in his or her state's best interests. Their efforts may not always succeed especially when a majority in the state legislature belongs to one political party and the governor is the leader of the other party. Governors also prepare the **budget**, a yearly plan that shows how much money the state intends to spend on its programs, equipment, and employees and how much money the state will take in from taxes, fees, and grants from the national government. Before the legislators approve the budget by turning it into law, they often make changes the governor might not like, just as they do with other laws.

The governors do not have to accept these changes. In all states except North Carolina, the governor can **veto** a bill by refusing to sign it into law or by letting it sit on his or her desk unsigned for ten days if meanwhile the legislative session ends. These are powers similar to those of the president of the United States. Governor Mario Cuomo repeatedly vetoed laws to impose the death penalty for certain crimes in New York State (thirty-six states and the national government have such **capital punishment** laws). Vetoed bills can still become law if two-thirds of the legislators in each house pass them again. The New

New York Governor Mario Cuomo has used his power to veto on several death penalty bills passed by the New York state legislature.

York state legislature, however, has not succeeded in getting a two-thirds majority to support the death penalty. In forty-seven states, governors also have **item vetoes**, which allow them to cross out specific parts of spending bills they think are faulty. This is an important power the president of the United States wishes he had.

Like the president, governors can make laws on their own without going to the state legislatures. They issue **executive orders**. This power can come from state constitutions, specific laws, or just from their general powers as chief executives of their states. The orders allow governors to fill in details of the broad and general laws state legislatures sometimes pass or to create committees to advise them and provide them with information they need. Executive orders are also issued when a state faces a natural disaster, such as a hurricane or earthquake, and action must be taken at once.

Among the states, there are also different ways in which governors exercise their judicial powers. They may grant pardons to individuals convicted of violating state laws or amnesty to prisoners. In half of the states, governors consult with pardoning boards before they act; the governors make these decisions on their own in the rest of the states. Congress has given governors the responsibility of returning escaped criminals who cross into their states, however at times, governors have refused to turn over these people. A famous example occurred in 1948, when the governor of Michigan, G. Mennon Williams, turned down Alabama's request to hand over one of the "Scottsboro boys." These were nine black youths imprisoned in 1931 for a crime many people felt they had not committed.

The number of officials governors can appoint to manage state government varies from state to state. Usually, these appointments require the approval of state senates. The governors of Mississippi, South Carolina, and Texas can give out fewer jobs than the governors of other states. Overall, the governors' power to appoint state officials is limited because state constitutions provide that as many as eight statewide posts may be elective.

Forty-two states elect lieutenant governors, who may not even belong to the same political party as the governor or share the governor's political opinions. Yet, like the vice president of the United States, these officials take over the governor's responsibilities if governors leave the state, become severely disabled, or die. In 1980, Lieutenant Governor William O'Neill became the governor of Connecticut when Ella Grasso resigned because of a fatal illness. O'Neill went on to be elected governor in his own right. Some lieutenant governors preside over the state senate or coordinate state departments. Others, however, have little to do since state law does not give them any official duties. Thus, in several small states, such as Nevada, the post is just a part-time job.

In forty-three states, voters elect the **attorney general**, who represents the state in legal cases and supervises local prosecutors. The **state treasurer**, in charge of the state's money, is elected in thirty-eight states. Voters pick the **secretary of state** in thirty-six states; this official publishes laws and supervises elections. Sixteen states make the **superintendent** or **commissioner of education** an elected position. Since these officeholders do not depend on the governors for their jobs, they can act independently of him. This is why governors do not always control the management of state affairs.

As chief executives, the governors' most important responsibility is putting state laws into effect. They appoint the heads of departments and agencies who help them supervise state employees. Across the nation there are at least 4.8 million state employees. These employees often must take competitive exams as part of their job applications. They perform important duties such as testing new automobile drivers, recording and storing birth certificates, making

Governors are responsible for calling upon the state National Guard in times of natural disaster or civil unrest.

sure the highways are in good repair, and distributing funds to unemployed workers. When these employees sometimes go on strike for higher pay, Americans truly understand all the vital work that they do.

Governors also serve as commanders-in-chief of the states' National Guard. They can call upon the troops to save lives and protect property during

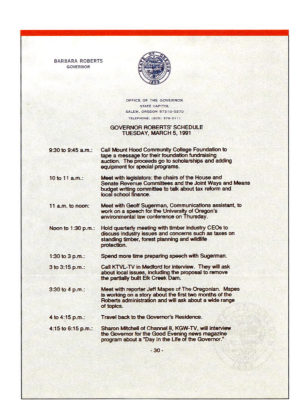

BARBARA ROBERTS
GOVERNOR

OFFICE OF THE GOVERNOR
STATE CAPITOL
SALEM, OREGON 97310-0370
TELEPHONE: (503) 378-3111

**GOVERNOR ROBERTS' SCHEDULE
TUESDAY, MARCH 5, 1991**

9:30 to 9:45 a.m.: Call Mount Hood Community College Foundation to tape a message for their foundation fundraising auction. The proceeds go to scholarships and adding equipment for special programs.

10 to 11 a.m.: Meet with legislators: the chairs of the House and Senate Revenue Committees and the Joint Ways and Means budget writing committee to talk about tax reform and local school finance.

11 a.m. to noon: Meet with Geoff Sugerman, Communications assistant, to work on a speech for the University of Oregon's environmental law conference on Thursday.

Noon to 1:30 p.m.: Hold quarterly meeting with timber industry CEOs to discuss industry issues and concerns such as taxes on standing timber, forest planning and wildlife protection.

1:30 to 3 p.m.: Spend more time preparing speech with Sugerman.

3 to 3:15 p.m.: Call KTVL-TV in Medford for interview. They will ask about local issues, including the proposal to remove the partially built Elk Creek Dam.

3:30 to 4 p.m.: Meet with reporter Jeff Mapes of The Oregonian. Mapes is working on a story about the first two months of the Roberts administration and will ask about a wide range of topics.

4 to 4:15 p.m.: Travel back to the Governor's Residence.

4:15 to 6:15 p.m.: Sharon Mitchell of Channel 8, KGW-TV, will interview the Governor for the Good Evening news magazine program about a "Day in the Life of the Governor."

- 30 -

An example of the busy schedule of Oregon Governor Barbara Roberts.

natural disasters, riots, or other civil disturbances. Governors can also use the state police in such situations. In September 1957, Arkansas Governor Orval E. Faubus ordered his state's National Guard to prevent nine black students from attending all-white Central High School in Little Rock. Angry mobs assembled at the school screaming racial insults and threats at the nine students. To make sure the students could safely go to school, the national government sent the 101st Airborne Division to Little Rock to protect them.

Governors in forty-seven states are given four-year terms. In Rhode Island, Vermont, and New Hampshire, however, governors hold office for only two years. In 1991, people in Vermont and Rhode Island began discussing proposals to extend their governors' terms. In both states, this requires a state constitutional amendment. Whether the changes are made remains to be seen. So far, thirteen women have served as governors, and in 1991, Virginia elected the nation's first black governor, L. Douglas Wilder. Many governors, such as Thomas Jefferson, Grover Cleveland, Jimmy Carter, and Ronald Reagan, have gone on to become Presidents of the United States.

Governors find that their jobs offer them much variety because they are expected to serve their state in so many different ways. Within the fifty states, there is also a wide range of powers given to individual governors and differences in the way they are allowed to use them. Every state varies in size, geographic location, and economic activities, so it makes sense for the states, and not a central government, to decide what they want their governors to be able to do.

It took a state Supreme Court decision to allow girls to play on Little League teams with boys.

Chapter Four

THE JUDICIARY:

Multiple Court Systems
Settling Disputes

In the past, only boys, ages eight to twelve, were allowed to join Little League baseball teams. Girls in the same age group were encouraged to play softball instead. Then in 1974, eight girls from Teaneck, New Jersey, decided that they wanted to become members of their local Little League team. When they were turned down, a women's rights group asked New Jersey government officials for help. The state officials decided to look into the matter. They heard experts on child health and development offer opinions about girls' fitness to play baseball. The officials soon became convinced that girls in the eight-to-twelve age group were equal in athletic ability to boys of the same age and faced no greater risk of injury playing baseball than the boys. So the officials issued an order to let girls join the Little League.

The Little League hired lawyers who challenged this decision. They took the case to the Superior Court of New Jersey, but the court decided in favor of the state officials. The judges ordered all Little League teams in New Jersey to admit girls into their baseball programs. Since then, Little League teams in all fifty states have become coeducational. In 1989, a girl even took part in the Little League World Series, and a woman served as an umpire for the first time.

State courts are an important part of the American legal system. They apply **civil law** when they decide most of the lawsuits involving private individuals or businesses. They also judge people accused of breaking the state's **criminal laws**. The courts sometimes make decisions that affect the way a state goes about its business. As the Little League case shows, their judgments can even change rules so that more people have an opportunity to take part in activities that matter to them.

States organize their court systems in several different ways. Most states have minor courts in both rural areas and cities to handle simple legal problems, such as disputes over speeding tickets. For more serious crimes or lawsuits involving large sums of money, cases are heard in general trial courts, which are known by a variety of different names: county courts, superior courts, district courts, courts

A judge addresses his court in Rockville, Maryland.

of common pleas. These courts handle most of the criminal cases in the nation.

To complicate matters, some states have separate trial courts for civil and criminal cases. States may also have special courts, such as juvenile courts, domestic relations courts, and probate courts. Juvenile courts deal with children too young to go through

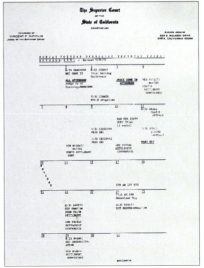

Top, the Supreme Court of the state of Texas; inset, California Superior Court Judge Di Figlia's day begins early and is often spent entirely in the courtroom trying cases.

the regular court system. Domestic relations courts take up legal problems among family members. **Probate courts** manage the legal and financial affairs of people who have died to make sure that their last wishes, usually written in their wills, are carried out.

In most states, lawyers can ask **appeals courts** to review trial court judgments and state officials' rulings to make sure that the decisions were fair, as was done in the Little League case. In eight states that do not have appeals courts, appeals from trial courts go directly to the highest state court, sometimes called a supreme court. All fifty states have a high court that can review decisions the appeals courts have made. These high courts are also known by a variety of names. For example, the highest court in Maine is called the Supreme Judicial Court; in Maryland, the Court of Appeals. In Oklahoma and Texas, there are two high courts: a Supreme Court for civil disputes and a Court of Criminal Appeals for criminal cases. All 28,000 state judges take an oath to obey the Constitution of the United States and the constitution of their state. When deciding a lawsuit, if they find that a state law violates either constitution, they may set it aside under the power of **judicial review**—an examination of the actions of state officials and the contents of state laws to make sure that they agree with the rules of government written in a constitution. The judge's decisions may be appealed to the highest state court for a final review. State judges may also have to apply national laws to state lawsuits. Such cases may be appealed to the **Supreme Court** of the United States, the highest court in the land. There are three remedies for unpopular state court decisions: passing new laws, amending the state constitution, or electing new judges.

Unlike federal judges who are appointed to the United States courts, the states use four different methods of selecting judges. In most states, voters simply elect their judges along with other officials. Some states follow the Missouri Plan, first used in 1940, in which the governor names a judge, but his selection must be approved by the voters at the next general election. In some states, judges are chosen by the governor, whose choice is subject to the consent of state senates, rather than the voters. The fourth method is simply to have the state legislature elect all judges.

Why do we need so many methods of selecting judges? Some people prefer that governors and legislatures should select judges because the broad voting public lacks information needed to choose properly. Other people claim that allowing the people to elect their judges makes the judges more respon-

ED

JUDGE KEN
RILEY
SUPERIOR COURT

*Some judges are appointed,
while others must run for
office in general elections.*

sible to the people. This is probably why the fifty states have never settled on one method of choosing their judges.

In most states people vote for **prosecutors** as well as judges, although in Connecticut and New Jersey these county officials are appointed to office. There are about 18,000 state prosecutors in the nation. It is their job to decide whether to bring charges against individuals suspected of committing crimes and whether to bring cases against those individuals to trial. In court, they argue the state's case against people accused of crimes. Sometimes prosecutors are willing to reduce criminal charges if a suspect agrees to plead guilty to a less serious offense and avoid a lengthy and costly trial. This is called **plea bargaining**.

In addition to voting for judges and prosecutors, many citizens become involved with their state's legal system when they are asked to serve as a member of a **jury**. Juries, made up of from six to twelve people, are used most often in criminal cases. The jurors listen to the arguments and evidence presented by prosecutors and defense lawyers. If the individuals accused of crimes cannot afford a lawyer, the court will assign a **public defender** to represent them. After listening to the judge's instructions, as well as both sides of the case, the jury decides whether the accused person is guilty or innocent. If the verdict is guilty, the judge decides the proper punishment.

The number of people serving sentences in state prisons continues to increase each year. As a result, prisons are severely overcrowded. In about forty states, federal judges have issued orders to either improve conditions at once or release some of the prisoners. Since each prison cell costs nearly $100,000 to build, new prisons are expensive, too expensive for financially strapped states to erect. Instead some states are developing new programs for people who are not hardened criminals and have not committed violent crimes. They may be required to help those in need by performing community service, or they may be placed in **half-way houses**, where they live under strict supervision but are allowed to go to work.

The state governments organize their courts in many different ways. There is no common method for selecting judges. The judges do not always reach the same conclusions when they decide similar cases. When there is a need for uniformity, the federal courts step in and make rulings that apply to all fifty states. Otherwise, each state is free to interpret and judge its own laws in its own way. So there are many advantages to having fifty state court systems as well as a federal system of justice.

Different states have different personalities, needs, philosophies, even geographies. Can you think of ways in which Oregon's Ecola State Park (top) might be managed differently than Idaho's Sandy Point State Park (bottom)?

Chapter Five

VARIATIONS AMONG STATES

Necessary and Desirable

There are many reasons why all fifty states cannot be governed in the same way. For instance, every state has its own individual history and, therefore, differing values and laws. Thirteen states in the Northeast helped form the national government. Pioneers moving westward created states out of territories originally occupied by American Indians. Other states (such as Louisiana, Florida, and Alaska) were carved out of lands purchased from foreign governments and settled by their peoples. At one time, Texas and Hawaii were even independent nations.

The fifty states do not share a common climate or similar landforms—consider the differences among snowy Alaska, sunny Hawaii, the Nevada deserts, and the Colorado mountains. The uneven distribution of natural resources creates yet other differences among the states: Oklahoma and Texas produce oil; Oregon and Washington produce lumber; Pennsylvania and West Virginia mine coal; and Kansas and Nebraska grow wheat.

People are not evenly distributed throughout the states either. California has the largest population; Alaska, the smallest. Nor does every state have the same mixture of religions, ages, cultures, and races. Utah has the most Mormons; Florida, the most elderly and retirees; New York, the most Puerto Ricans; Mississippi, the most African Americans.

When we consider all these differences, it's no wonder that people in each state have different needs and interests. The states cannot be expected to simply pass identical laws for their citizens' health, safety, and welfare. For example, thirty-one states require people to have blood tests for certain diseases before they can obtain licenses to marry. Thirty-six states impose the death penalty for certain categories of crimes. Even when states have similar programs, differences still exist. While all states spend money to educate elementary and high school students, Alaska spends the most money per pupil, while Utah spends the least.

In 1989, President George Bush (right) attended an education summit where many state governors gathered to discuss their states' different needs. President Bush is shown greeting Iowa Governor Terry Branstad (center) and Arkansas Governor Bill Clinton (left). Three years later, Clinton unseated Bush as President of the United States.

State legislatures regulate where people are allowed to smoke, as well as determine at what age young people may smoke.

Differences among the states are vital to all Americans. Not only do they allow adjustments for various local conditions and needs, they also offer states the chance to experiment with alternative ways of doing things. If the experiments are successful, other states, or even the national government, may copy them. For example, in 1869, Wyoming became the first state to allow women to vote in elections. By 1900, four other states had passed similar laws, and within twenty years the national government had given women the right to vote. In 1991, Iowa became the first state to make it illegal for anyone under the age of eighteen to smoke cigarettes, imposing a $100 fine for the offense. Forty-four other states only have laws banning cigarette sales to minors. Many anti-smoking advocates hope that Iowa's law will be adopted by the rest of the states, as well as the national government.

The national government provides a common policy for all the people when needed. It is certainly more convenient to have a standard money system than for each state to make its own coins and give them separate values. Over the years, the national government has passed uniform laws when differences in state laws proved unfair to large numbers of citizens or posed a heavy burden on some states. This is why the national government pays for food

Legal and medical assistance for poor citizens is yet another obligation of state governments.

stamp programs and aid to the disabled and the old.

The national government also encourages the states to participate in certain activities. It offers money to them to encourage them to build highways, hospitals, and schools, to help families with needy children, and to assist those too poor to pay the costs of their health care. The states must usually put up some money of their own to match these funds. They must also meet certain federal standards in using the money. However, the states are free to accept these programs or turn them down.

By having such a variety of state governments and programs as well as a national government which sets common standards, Americans are able to enjoy the benefits of diversity and unity. They have the opportunity to learn from experience, to grow, and to change.

Glossary

amendments—Formal changes that add to or subtract from state constitutions.

appeals courts—Review trial court judgments and state officials' ruling to make sure the proper procedures were followed and the decisions were fair.

attorney general—Represents the state in legal cases and supervises local prosecutors.

Bill of Rights—Guarantees citizens their basic freedoms, such as the right to free speech.

bills—Proposed laws.

budget—A yearly plan showing how much money the state intends to spend on its programs, equipment, and employees, and how much money the state will take in from taxes and fees, as well as from grants from the national government.

capital punishment—The death penalty, which is imposed for the most serious crimes.

civil law—Applied by courts mostly to decide the lawsuits involving private individuals or businesses.

conference committee—Made up of members from each house of the state legislature and used to settle differences between alternative versions of the same bill, passed in each house.

Congress—The national legislature, made up of two chambers: the 435-member House of Representatives, and the 100-member Senate.

Constitution—Defines the duties of the national government and the states and limits their powers. It also creates a special partnership between the states and the national government.

constitutional conventions—Special meetings to rewrite completely state constitutions.

criminal law—Applied by courts to people accused of crimes.

electoral college—Formed by the states every four years to help elect the president after the voters have chosen their winner.

executive—The branch of state government that carries out the laws under the direction of the governor.

executive orders—Permits governors to make laws by

themselves without the specific approval of the state legislatures. Sometimes, these orders let governors fill in details when state legislatures pass broad and general laws.

extradite—To return prisoners from one state who flee into another state. The Constitution encourages governors to extradite these fugitives so that no state becomes a safe haven for individuals wanted in another state.

federalism—A special partnership between the national and state governments that divides power between states and the national government and allows both levels of government to make laws for the people.

half-way houses—Where people convicted of nonviolent crimes might be sentenced rather than prison. In half-way houses, people live under strict supervision but are let out to go to work.

impeachment—A two-step process that gives state legislatures the power to accuse formally public officials of wrongdoing and to remove them from office if necessary.

initiative petition—Allows citizens to suggest amendments and laws for voters to accept or reject at election time. The petitions must contain signatures of from five to fifteen percent of all the people who voted in the last election.

interstate compacts—Voluntary agreements among

the states, made with the approval of Congress, that concern such matters as common management of waterways, transportation, and environmental protection.

item vetoes—Allow governors to reject specific parts of spending bills. The president of the United States does not have this power.

joint committees—These committees, made up of members of both houses of a state legislature, speed up the legislative process by weeding out the weakest bills and leaving the rest to be introduced in one house or the other.

judicial review—Examining the actions of state officials and the contents of state laws to make sure that they agree with the rules of government in a constitution.

judiciary—The branch of state government made up of courts where judges decide disputes about laws and try lawbreakers.

juries—Six to twelve people who listen to the arguments and evidence by the prosecutors and defense lawyers. After listening to the judge's instructions about the law, they decide whether the accused person is innocent or guilty. Juries are used most often in criminal cases.

legislature—The branch of state government which makes laws.

plea bargaining—Reducing criminal charges if a suspect agrees to plead guilty to a less serious offense.

political parties—Organizations that get people to run for office in elections.

probate courts—Manage the affairs of people who have died to make sure that their last wishes, usually written in their wills, are carried out.

prosecutors—Decide whether to bring charges against individuals suspected of committing crimes and whether to bring those cases to trial. In court, they argue the state's case against people accused of crimes.

public defender—Assigned by the court to represent people accused of crimes who cannot afford a lawyer.

recall—A special election enabling voters to remove state (or local) officials from office.

redistricting—Having state legislatures draw up plans after each census to make adjustments in number and boundaries of the legislative districts that elect representatives to the state and national legislature.

referendum—An opportunity for the public to approve or reject laws by voting on them at the next general election.

residency requirements—The amount of time (usually one year) a person must spend living in a state before receiving the full benefits of state citizenship.

secretary of state—This official publishes laws and supervises elections in most states.

standing committees—Permanent groups, divided by subject matter, within the state legislature. They study proposed laws, hold hearings, and may make changes in wording and contents of these bills. Then, if a majority of the committee supports a particular bill, it is sent along to the entire house to be made into a law.

state treasurer—An official who is in charge of the state's money.

sunset laws—Rules requiring state agencies to explain why they should be continued after six or seven years. In this way state legislatures can get rid of useless projects and set up new programs.

Supreme Court of the United States—The highest court in the land.

veto—The procedure that lets governors turn down a law by refusing to sign it or by letting it sit on their desk unsigned for ten days while the legislature ends its session.

For further reading

Batchelor, John E. *States' Rights.* New York: Franklin Watts, 1986.

Bernotas, Jr., Bob. *Federal Government: How It Works.* New York: Chelsea House, 1990.

Bernstein, Richard & Jerome Angel. *Congress.* New York: Walker & Co., 1989.

Feinberg, Barbara Silberdick. *The Constitution: Yesterday, Today, and Tomorrow.* New York: Scholastic, Inc., 1987.

Green, Carl & William Sanford. *Congress.* Vero Beach, FL: Rourke Corp, 1990.

Jenkins, George. *Constitution.* Vero Beach, FL: Rourke Corp.,1990.

Lindop, Edmund. *The Bill of Rights and Landmark Cases.* New York: Franklin Watts, 1989.

Lindop, Edmund. *Presidents by Accident.* New York: Franklin Watts, 1991.

Mabie, Margot. *Constitution: Reflection of a Changing Nation.* New York: Henry Holt & Co., 1987.

McPhillips, Martin. *Constitutional Convention.* Morristown, NJ: Silver, Burdett & Ginn, 1986.

Ragsdale, Bruce A. *House of Representatives.* New York: Chelsea House, 1989.

Ritchie, Donald A. *Senate.* New York: Chelsea House, 1988.

Index

About the Author

Barbara Silberdick Feinberg graduated with honors from Wellesley College and holds a Ph.D. in political science from Yale University. Among her books for Franklin Watts are *Marx and Marxism, Watergate: Scandal in the White House*, and *American Political Scandals Past and Present*. She is currently preparing a student's dictionary of American government and politics and a biography of President Harry Truman, to be published in September 1993.

Mrs. Feinberg lives in New York with her two sons, Jeremy and Douglas, and a Yorkshire terrier named Katie.

DATE			